The Pocket Screenwriting Guide

120 Tips for Getting to FADE OUT

By Mario O. Moreno and Anthony Grieco

The Writers Store®, Inc.

Copyright © 2009 The Writers Store, Inc.

All rights reserved. Except as permitted under the U.S. Copyright Act of 1976, no part of this publication may be reproduced, distributed, or transmitted in any form or by any means, or stored in a database or retrieval system, without prior written permission of the publisher.

The Writers Store, Inc.
2040 Westwood Blvd.
Los Angeles, CA 90025

310.441.5151

ISBN Number: 978-0-615-32609-2

Printed in the United States of America

Contents

Introduction	1
Additional Resources	3
How to Use This Book	5
120 Screenwriting Tips	7
Screenwriting Terminology Guide	70
Recommended Books for Further Reading	105

Introduction

Since 1982, professional and aspiring scribes have looked to us at The Writers Store as trustworthy experts on all matters related to screenwriting. It's been our passion to continually seek out the best and most up-to-date answers to the many queries we receive on a daily basis.

This handy little guide serves as the culmination of our many years in the Industry. In it you'll find 120 tips on plot, structure, character and mythology that give you a constant point of reference while you write.

Good luck, and happy writing!

Additional Resources

Screenwriting Pro
Screenwriting software that's ready for action

Web-based Screenwriting Pro is a complete script-formatting solution for feature films, television and plays that represents a huge step forward for writers and filmmakers. With no software to install and no technical matters like upgrades to deal with, Screenwriting Pro frees you to focus on what really matters: writing the screenplay.

It has all the elements you look for in boxed scriptwriting software, including Industry-standard formatting as you type, story development tools and a library of templates, with the added benefit of working online from any Internet-connected computer. Go to ScreenwritingPro.com now to see how this application can revolutionize the way you write scripts.

The Writers Store
Essentials for writers & filmmakers

The Writers Store has been respected worldwide as the leading authority on writing and filmmaking wares since 1982, with an ever-advancing roster of services, books, software, supplies and events. Their specially trained team, The Story Specialists, can guide you to the perfect product to make you a master of the craft.

Visit WritersStore.com and be sure to sign up for the free eZine, filled with tips and expert articles. You can also reach The Writers Store by phone at 800.272.8927. The Story Specialists are waiting to speak to you about your project now!

How to Use This Book

The Pocket Screenwriting Guide is designed to lead you through Hollywood screenplay structure from beginning to end. While the 120 pointers that form its foundation do not directly correlate page-by-page to a standard 2-hour script, they are arranged in the order of classic storytelling construction.

The tips are also broken down into 4 categories marked with symbols, allowing you to refer to them at any point in the writing process:

- **Sequences** 🎞
   A film can be broken into quarters, with each quarter (approximately 20-30 minutes) being split into two Sequences.

- **Major Beats** ♪
   Each Sequence peaks with a Major Beat that shifts the story into the next Sequence.

- **Pivotal Moments** ⚙☼
   Aside from Sequences and Major Beats, Pivotal Moments like "Meet the Opposing Force," and "Hint the Soul" can be used based on the needs of the story.

- **General Tips** 💡
  Pointers on description, dialogue, and writing in general.

Further, the Pocket Screenwriting Guide features a handy "AKA" section, listing the different names given to a particular element in the screenwriting process by popular authors and instructors. For easier reading, the third person singular is used in masculine form throughout the text.

The tips contained in this guide, compiled by the authors over the course of many years in the screenwriting industry, were not easy to come by. Some emerged as epiphanies during the writing and rewriting process while others were culled from the notes of agents, managers and executives. The rest came from Hollywood word-of-mouth and the reading of books that refer to the same elements by different names.

It's your choice how to apply the theories presented in this book to your story. But with the knowledge you glean, you'll be able to craft a compelling story, filled with subtext and deeper meaning.

120 Screenwriting Tips

1. FADE IN IMAGE 🎵

What is the first image the audience sees when the story starts? The Fade In Image can be an object (or objects) symbolic to your story, the tone, the location, the Lead Character, the Opposing Force, or even a mysterious visual clue. Sound can play a large part, whether alone or in conjunction with a visual.

This is not the first decision you need to make. It may be the last or second-to-last (with the FADE OUT IMAGE). Ideally the "beginning and ending" or "opening and closing" should match or reflect each other, and end up being the bookends of your story.

2. WORLD OF THE STORY 🎞

AKA: Set-Up / Ordinary World / Point of Attack / Sequence A / Mini-Movie 1

The first ten to twenty pages of your script should introduce the World in which the story takes place. What city? What time period? What part of society? What tone? You can also show the Lead's life at home, work, and play – in whatever order suits the story best.

You should also establish the rules specific to this reality, especially if your World has any sort of supernatural elements. For example, "This is a World where superheroes live and are liable for prosecution" or "This is a World where people can do magic" and so on.

By setting up your World, leaps that you might take later can be established now, and won't seem contrived or out-of-the-blue.

3. MEET THE LEAD ⚙⚙

AKA: Protagonist / Central Character / Hero / Heroine / Archetype / Antihero / Star / Good Guy / Main Character

The Lead is the central person the story is about. Although circumstances will occur that are out of his control, he will lead the plot by his internal reactions, decisions, and actions.

To convey the feeling of real life, try to introduce the Lead in the middle of an action, trying to do or obtain something. The classical Greeks, and most books on writing for the screen, refer to this as *In Media Res*. This action won't be what the Lead is trying to accomplish throughout the film, but rather an introduction of him actively inhabiting the World.

How well you do this will reflect greatly on how the audience perceives the Lead throughout the script.

4. CHOOSING THE RIGHT LEAD 💡

Make sure you know who your Lead is and that the story will be told through his eyes. Oftentimes, the trick to telling the best possible story is to tell it from the right character's point of view.

Frank Capra once said, "The whole thing is, you've got to make them care about somebody."

5. INTRODUCING MAJOR CHARACTERS 💡

When we first meet a character, we CAPITALIZE his whole name (I.E. JOHN SMITH), include age (if necessary) and give brief information about him (preferably visual).

You don't have to tell us what hair or eye color he has or how tall he is, unless it is pertinent to the story. We just want an idea of who we are watching.

Here's an example from Frank Darabont's *The Shawshank Redemption*:

```
ANDY DUFRESNE, mid-20s, wire rim
glasses, three-piece suit. Under
normal circumstances a respectable,
solid citizen; hardly dangerous,
perhaps even meek.
```

And one from Cameron Crowe's *Almost Famous*:

```
Moving into the parking lot light
is a luminous girl in a green faux-
fur trimmed coat.  This is PENNY
LANE.  There is an inviting warmth
and real interest as she asks:

          PENNY
     ... you're not a what?
```

6. THE LEAD'S SPECIALTY ⚙⚙

Ask yourself: "What makes the Lead special?"

The Lead doesn't have to have a super power, but everyone has some sort of talent. Great lover, fighter, driver, chef, crook, hacker, artist, student, detective, athlete, parent, dreamer, gambler, scientist, friend...etc. It's what we are, what we do, and what we care about.

This will frequently be the only tool the Lead has to help him deal with what's about to come.

It's important to show what makes your Lead unique because the audience wants to know why this person is worth watching and rooting for.

Think of it like meeting someone at a party. If there doesn't seem to be anything interesting about the person, do you want to get to know him better?

7. THE LEAD'S FLAW ⚙⚙

People aren't perfect. Stories about people without any flaws seem unrealistic or flat.

In Jungian psychology, a person's flaw is referred to as the "shadow." Get in touch with your shadow and let that feed your character.

Some of the most memorable characters in film history are remembered primarily for their shadow. For example, Charles Foster Kane's unquenchable ambition in *Citizen Kane*, Jake La Motta's violent temper in *Raging Bull*, Fletcher Reede's lying in *Liar, Liar*, and Shrek's selfishness in *Shrek*.

Often the Lead doesn't know he has a major flaw, but events in the story force him to come face-to-face with it, and usually require him to overcome that flaw in order to succeed.

8. HINT THE SOUL ⚙☼
AKA: Theme / Premise / Idea / Thesis / Argument / Message / Core / Truth / Spine

The Soul is the heart of the story. It gives value to your story's existence and serves as the lifeblood that keeps all the separate elements together. Your characters and conflicts must prove this idea, whatever it is.

Scenes, sequences, and character decisions have the potential to work in many different ways. This brings the risk of losing the track of the story, because the writer will often choose to follow whatever approach comes first, even if it's not the best choice for the overall piece. To keep focus and guide your decisions, know what it really is you want to say. You need to find that pulse.

To figure out your story's Soul, ask yourself, "What is the reason I want to tell this story, what deeper meaning does all this hold for me?"

Your story's Soul can be chosen from an array of classic human topics including: Love, War, Family, Faith, Politics, Friendship, Jealousy, Power, Duty, Corruption, Self-Awareness, or Justice. Choose the Soul that elicits an emotional and visceral response in you. Your experiences, instincts, and world view are what you, and only you, can bring to any given story – its DNA code.

The Soul of the story is not normally stated by the Lead. A supporting character, sometimes in the form of a Theme Character who reiterates the Soul at various times over the course of the story, will usually hint the Soul in an off-hand manner, or else the Soul should appear as subtext.

If the Soul is in place, you will never hear the question "What is this story really about?"

9. TOO MUCH TV 💡

Try to avoid starting a script with your Lead on the couch watching TV or sitting at a bar. It is best to find our Lead in action. It provides an opportunity to establish a skill, besides sloth or drunkenness.

10. MEET THE OPPOSING FORCE ⚙⚙
AKA: Antagonist / Villain / Opposition / Adversary / Bad Guy

The Opposing Force can be a person, group, or larger natural (or supernatural) force. Opposing Forces tend to see themselves as the Lead of their own story, so they also have a back-story, bringing them to where they are now.

An Opposing Force needs to be a multi-dimensional character, and have a specific goal, not because of the evil that can be caused, but for some personal or financial reason.

Some Opposing Forces are the exact opposite of the Lead character, like two sides of the same coin. They can embody the Lead's shadow at its worst.

Opposing Forces can illustrate the negative argument of the theme, so if the Lead succeeds against them at the end, he's proving the theme. If the Lead fails to gain what he wants at the end, this also makes a statement about the theme.

11. THE SMALL DEATH ⚙⚙

When a story starts, the Lead has either accepted the World he lives in and believes nothing is wrong with it, or he pays lip service to changing it. The Lead will usually have a brief moment of clarity before his life changes, a moment in which he will see that his life is in neutral or stalled. This gives us hope for his ability to change.

12. THE SPARK 🎵
AKA: Catalyst / Inciting Incident / Call to Adventure / Life-Changing Event / The Problem / Hook

Stalled as it may be, the World is in balance for the Lead, usually for the wrong reasons, and then something happens, the Spark, which throws everything off. It sets up all that will follow and it presents the Lead with a challenge that he will have to overcome. The rest of the story becomes about finding a way to restore or find new balance.

13. DELIBERATION 🎞️
AKA: Refusal of the Call / Debate / Sequence B / Mini-Movie 2

The Lead tries to go about his normal life, but can't because of what has changed, forcing him to reexamine the position the Spark has put him in.

Usually, when the Lead is first presented with this challenge, he refuses to face it. He'll turn it down, thinking he can ignore it, or he'll wonder whether he is up to the caliber of handling such a problem.

If he thinks he can handle it, chances are others will doubt the Lead's ability. Whether this is the case or not, the odds are against the Lead being prepared, until a twist turns the plot in a new direction, or it becomes painfully, dreadfully, unavoidably obvious that action must be taken. This sequence peaks with "The Big Step."

14. SHOW, DON'T TELL 💡

Screenwriting is a visual medium. A character's behavior and his actions are more important than what he says. Try NOT to express all that is happening through dialogue.

15. INTRODUCING MINOR CHARACTERS 💡

When introducing secondary characters who have one or two lines, such as MAN #1, try to be descriptive and creative, and introduce them as HEAVY MAN, for instance. Instead of COP #1, try OLD COP, or TALL COP.

16. THE FOUR-LINE PRINCIPLE FOR DESCRIPTION (the Rule of Thumb) 💡

Try to limit descriptive passages to no more than three or four lines, or about the size of the top half of your thumb. Nothing turns readers off more than having to work their way through large chunks of description. You can get across a lot of visual and emotional information with fewer words in a script. The best ways to learn this craft are to read scripts, write scripts, and rewrite scripts.

And remember, a screenplay is a blueprint for a film, not a book. It will constantly be in flux, like a living thing, all the way through production and even into the editing room, so the goal is to make sure you're telling the story clearly.

17. THE RULE OF THUMB FOR DIALOGUE

A great test for dialogue is to keep it no longer than two or three sentences, or two fingers thick in length. Longer diatribes fall flat and are unnatural, killing the flow. Long passages work better with rants or public speeches. But even then, cut away to reaction shots, especially to your Lead if he's not speaking.

18. LENGTH OF SCENES

Try to keep scenes no longer than 3 pages, and see if you can keep most under two. Remember, each page equals about a minute of screen time – which can seem like forever in the dark.

19. AVOIDING CHARACTER NAME CONFUSION 💡

Avoid having characters whose names start with the same letter, or rhyme, unless done with a specific intent.

For example, Stacy, Stevie and Sherri should not all be in the same script. Readers often do not read your script in one straight go. They might need to take breaks or get distracted by life. Clarity is their friend.

20. NOUNS 💡

Describe nouns by their specific names. Instead of gun, try Colt, Magnum or Carbine. Again, you are painting pictures. This is your opportunity to be specific without being wordy.

21. VERBS 💡

Use high-energy and emotionally evocative verbs. Instead of always using the verb "walk" use synonyms that capture your character's mood or behavior like saunter, amble or march.

22. BREVITY IS THE… 💡

The faster the read, the better. If you can use a one-syllable word over a four-syllable word, do it. You are creating a blueprint for many talented people who will color in the details for you.

23. DESCRIBING ENVIRONMENTS 💡

Instead of simply describing the environment, describe how the characters interact with it. You might imagine thirty chairs in a room, but if they don't affect the scene, there's no need to mention them.

24. THE READER'S EYE IS A CAMERA 💡

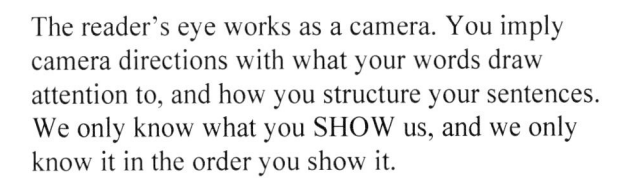

The reader's eye works as a camera. You imply camera directions with what your words draw attention to, and how you structure your sentences. We only know what you SHOW us, and we only know it in the order you show it.

For instance, if you start a scene by describing a person's face and then move to his general surroundings, the camera in a reader's mind does the same: it'll move from a close up of the face to a wide shot of the room.

25. CONTROL PACING THROUGH SENTENCE STRUCTURE 💡

You can control the reader's pace through the length of paragraphs and sentences. Clipped sentences read faster – best for action sequences or thrillers. Sentences with commas seem to flow slower, and can create mood, a great method used for dramas.

26. KEEP THE LEAD ACTIVE 💡

Make sure your Lead is always acting and reacting, right or wrong – especially when he is provoked and entering the second act. Secondary characters should not determine outcomes, but rather help move the Lead along.

27. THE POWER OF CONTRAST 💡

To contrast is to distinguish two things by comparing their differences, especially when they're opposites. You can use contrast in various ways in a screenplay; you can contrast a character with his environment, or with other characters, or even with how his inner feelings relate to his outer behavior.

For instance, when you look at characters in contrast to their environment, take a look at Elle at an Ivy League Law school in *Legally Blonde*, male musicians Joe and Jerry joining an all-girl band in

Some Like it Hot, Neo in *The Matrix*, or Marty McFly navigating 1955 in *Back to the Future*.

For character contrasts, examine Leads and Opposing Forces like Luke and Darth Vader in *Star Wars*, love interests like Harry and Sally, partners like Riggs and Murtaugh in *Lethal Weapon*, or even the various members of a team, like in *Ocean's Eleven*.

When looking at the contrast between a character's inner and outer behavior, study Bruce Wayne/Batman in *The Dark Knight*, Michael as Dorothy in *Tootsie*, Vincent Vega torn between loyalty to his boss and his attraction to his boss's wife in *Pulp Fiction*, or Michael Corleone's original wishes and ultimate actions in *The Godfather*.

28. THE BIG STEP 🎵
AKA: First Plot Point / First Turning Point / Peak of Act One / Act One Curtain / Crossing the First Threshold / Break Into Two

The Lead realizes that in spite of whatever doubts he or others may have, there is no choice but to deal with the challenge posed by the Spark and its aftermath.

The problem could be even worse than first thought. This is ideal for dramatic escalation. Something needs to be done. Action must be taken. Like it or not, the Lead now commits to taking it.

This moves the Lead to the next phase of his journey.

The Act One curtain should be treated like a beat as the Lead decides to go on the journey, just as you would begin packing for a flight. It's not quite Act Two, but we know the next time we see the Lead, the journey will have begun.

29. STATE THE CENTRAL QUESTION ⚙️⚙️

The Central Question can be asked at any point during Act One, but it should be crystal clear by the end of the Act. Even if it's as plain as the nose on your face in early drafts (subtlety can be employed in later drafts and polishes) you should make sure that the question has been planted in the audience's minds.

This question will be the underlying force that keeps the story's central focus clear. It is equivalent to a statement like: "Will the Lead be able to overcome his inner flaw, along with external obstacles presented by the Opposing Force, and get what he wants - or will he fail to save whatever is at stake?"

For example, in *Forrest Gump* the Central Question could be: "Will Forrest ever win Jenny's heart and become more than just her friend?" In *Slumdog Millionaire* it would be "How can a slumdog like Jamal know the answers to the questions and will he be able to reunite with Latika?"

The stakes are a major factor in all this. What is at stake if the Lead fails needs to dangle in our minds. The bigger or more personal the stakes, the more intriguing the story.

Experienced writers design events so that the stakes increase as the plot progresses. This keeps everything intriguing and fresh, thus keeping the audience on the edge of their seats.

Even as the stakes rise, the Central Question tends to stay the same. Sometimes part of the question (most likely the inner flaw) will be answered, either at the end of the second act or the Climax, but the essence of the question needs to remain in place.

If your third act seems to drag, chances are you have already answered the Central Question, and there is nothing left to keep the story's focus clear.

30. CROSSING A THRESHOLD 💡

Consider a beat a Threshold as we enter the second act that preys on the Lead's flaw. It can help set the tone for what might lie ahead, and reaffirm that your Lead has some commitment to leaving the ordinary behind.

When looking at this as metaphor, Joseph Campbell often used the example of the Lead crossing a river toward the other side - the unknown.

31. THE LEAD'S EASIEST RECOURSE 🎬
AKA: Confrontation / Plan A and Plan B / Fun and Games / Promise of Premise / Special World / Tests, Allies, and Enemies / Sequence C / Mini-Movie 3

Like most people, the Lead tries to solve his problem using the easiest solution first. This is where we take the Lead (with his skills and his flaws) and watch him as he tries to deal with the dilemma at hand. Of course, the Lead's easiest recourse never solves the problem. If it did, there would be no story left to tell. The obstacles increase as the Lead tries the next available recourse; however this usually doesn't work either.

The promise of your Premise is also fulfilled here, with the genre-defining moments the audience came to see. These moments don't have to move the plot forward as much as the later scenes.

This section can run as a stream of scene series leading to the Midpoint. Other times, this area is split in half by a major beat usually referred to as "the Pinch" and a sequence called "the Stretch."

32. IRONY 💡

When one speaks of irony, it's owed to the fact that your Lead will be forced to go against what he has become comfortable with – his flaw. If your character has a difficult time meeting people, have him forced into social situations. If he is filled with guilt, have him encounter situations that remind him of his wrongdoings, etc.

Don't forget about irony.

33. SUBPLOTS ⚙⚙

Since Act One has just recently peaked with the Big Step, now is a good time to briefly release some of the audience's tension, the way a roller coaster would dip before the next loop. This can constitute cutting away from the Lead and meeting new characters.

Sometimes the Lead will meet someone new or turn to someone he knows we haven't seen yet, creating a subplot, which should be related to the central plot or reflect directly on it. These encounters can be woven in through the narrative, and provide an extra sense of dimension or layers.

Major relationships in your story, especially those pivotal ones a character might find at home or work, can be developed into subplots.

When thinking about supporting characters, just make sure they fit your story and have their own goals, so that they appear real and add conflict to scenes in which the Lead has to deal with them. You can also use them to explore different aspects of the Lead's personality.

Be aware that all supporting characters either help or hurt the Lead, and if they don't do either one, they may be superfluous to your story.

Ideally, a subplot will have a structure following the same principles as a primary story, but told quickly. What would constitute a sequence in the bigger story can be reduced to simply a scene or a beat within a subplot.

Although you may have introduced your subplots in Act One, this is a good time to briefly shift the focus to them.

34. THE WANDERER 💡

Even if your story isn't a "fish out of water" story, this is your "fish out of water" section. This is when your Lead explores a World he's not accustomed to and it's usually where his flaw is exposed. This is when he accumulates skills and learns lessons that will pay off for him later.

35. DON'T STOP HERE 💡

Don't stop here! If you are having second thoughts about the script or the story or your talent... If you are starting to wonder whether you should have written that other idea... If you think a couple of weeks off will help cure your writer's block... DON'T STOP HERE.

Go back and make sure your Central Question is clear, then remind yourself about whatever it is that motivated you to want to tell this story. Forget about everything else and write your heart out. When this draft is done, the euphoria of watching it print out will have made this all worthwhile, and fixing anything that was off will be a million times easier.

36. PASSIVE VOICE

Avoid the passive voice. Your prose should be immediate. It's happening as we read it.

Don't do this: Henry is leaning against the bar.
Do this: Henry leans against the bar.

37. FINDING THE TITLE

Your title often comes from the first half of your second act. Why? Because it is the most ironic part of your script and therefore offers the best example of your Premise.

38. RUNNERS

Runners are recurring beats, often seen as plants and payoffs. Try setting up running gags or recurring characters, phrases, motifs, props, or images – set ups and payoffs are very rewarding to read and watch, and weave a layer of consistency throughout a story.

Examples of motifs are the roses in *American Beauty*, the grains in *Witness*, Pinot Noir grapes in *Sideways*, and the eyes in *Crimes & Misdemeanors*.

Props include the rings in *The Lord of The Rings*, Harvey Dent's coin in *The Dark Knight*, and the horcruxes in the *Harry Potter* series.

Phrases are the "And why do we fall" question used at several points in *Batman Begins* and the reference that the rug "…really tied the room together" in *The Big Lebowski*.

Running gags include the Lead constantly getting his finger cut off in *Kiss Kiss Bang Bang*, and the preemptive "Spaceballs" merchandising in *Spaceballs*.

39. THE OLD "IN LATE, OUT EARLY" 💡

This is a surefire way to not be boring. Look to avoid small talk and mundane day-to-day dialogue, like hellos, goodbyes and talk of the weather. Assume all those conversations have already taken place. Scenes are about conflict. Your dialogue should reflect this.

Once a story is in motion, start scenes on the action, and get out before it's over. Get into scenes late, and get out the moment the scene's purpose has been completed.

Leave us wanting to turn the page.

One trick to accomplishing this is to use your hand to cover the first instance of dialogue in a scene, then see if you can start on the second one without losing the reader. If so, cover the second speech and continue on until you reach the dialogue we can't do without. You can use this trick working your way back from the end of a scene as well.

40. BUTTONS 💡

A Button is often the last line or visual beat in a scene that tells us where your character stands emotionally. It can be a joke, something that denotes irony, or resonates thematically. It punctuates the tone, and catapults us into the next scene, like pushing the "next" button – with a BANG!

41. TALKING HEADS 💡

Avoid talking heads - be cinematic. Movies allow us to capture behavior and context, not just dialogue. Try having your scenes take place in environments that make your characters active and let them move through their World, revealing more about them, instead of treating it like they are standing in front of backdrops. Give them some business, especially actions that give us subtext about the scene or who they are.

42. THE AX IN THE ROOM 💡

Much in relation to the previous tip, the ax in the room is the object that becomes the extension of the character's emotional state. Think of it as a prop with emotional weight. Imagine this: two characters stand in a white room without doors or windows. They talk about how to get out, and then talk some more. Boring.

Now, pretend a trap door opens in the ceiling and someone drops in an ax.

Suddenly, we have an object to hack at a wall. Now we have something they can fight over. And now we just might have a murder weapon. Get the picture? Look at your scenes closely. Is there an ax in the room?

43. A WRITER'S REGIMEN 💡

Establish a routine. Try aiming for a page count or a time limit when you sit down to write. For example, five pages or two hours, whichever comes first.

44. PROPER USE OF CONTINUOUS 💡

Continuous is only used when a scene is a continuation of the previous scene, like a character moving from one room to the next. It does not mean a separate scene is taking place somewhere else at the same time.

45. THE PINCH (A.K.A. THE WALL) 🎵

The more options that are exhausted, the more the Lead becomes aware he must be willing to try new things. This is also a good time to reestablish goals and stakes.

The Pinch may be the least obvious major beat of all, and the hardest to identify in films, but it can be a useful tool to navigate the murky waters that are the first half of Act Two.

46. STRETCH 🎞
AKA: Approaching the Innermost Cave / Sequence D / Mini-Movie 4

This is often the "moment of initial growth or change" for the Lead. He has to try something new or let go of something from the past, even if he is still not on the right path to solving the problem.

The stretch between the Pinch and the Midpoint (the next major beat) can also use a false ending structured to mirror the Climax. For example, if the story is about a knight harnessing the powers of a special sword to defeat a dragon, this is where the two forces meet face-to-face for the first time. The knight has not yet mastered using the sword, so the dragon wins. It lets us know the Lead still has some work to do before he'll be able to solve his problem.

If the story is about a rise and fall, this is where the rise reaches its zenith.

47. THE TEXT MESSAGE 💡

This is not about formatting text messages; that you can find in a formatting guide. This is a new trick that has been helping writers tighten their dialogue. When stuck on dialogue, try texting the dialogue back and forth with a friend to see how little is really needed.

48. DON'T MAKE IT EASY ON THE LEAD 💡

Try to have characters lie or withhold information from your Lead as much as possible. This goes back to maximizing the potential for conflict. You don't have to overdo it, but you don't want to under-execute it either.

The old Hollywood adage is that "if your character is thirsty, and just wants a drink of water, throw everything you can at him to keep him from quenching his thirst."

49. OH, VOICEOVERS 💡

When using voiceovers, do not describe what the audience already sees. Instead, use it only when you are adding a character's impression or thought of what we are seeing. Tell us something we wouldn't know through the visual, especially if it contradicts what we are seeing.

Look at how voiceover is used in films like *Goodfellas, Forrest Gump, Annie Hall, Manhattan, Apocalypse Now, Network, Taxi Driver, Amadeus, Sunset Blvd, American Beauty, Shawshank Redemption, Million Dollar Baby, Fight Club, Kiss Kiss Bang Bang,* and *Milk.*

50. THE MAGIC FORMULA FOR WRITING SCRIPTS 💡

"The secret to writing a screenplay is keeping your ass in the chair."
-Oliver Stone

ASS + CHAIR = PAGES

51. DIALECT IN DIALOGUE 💡

Avoid dialect in dialogue, or don't overdo. Readers do not want to work at deciphering words. Simply state in your description that a character speaks in an accent. The actor will do the rest.

52. WORDS IN OTHER LANGUAGES 💡

Underline or italicize foreign words and phrases when they appear. This lets the reader know that you did not make an error, but rather are calling attention to the word. Either choice for formatting is acceptable, but must be consistent throughout the script.

53. PUNCTUATION TOOLS 💡

Use an em dash (—) when a character's speech is interrupted. Use ellipses (…) when a character's dialogue trails off.

For example:

```
                STEVE
    I had no idea. If I'd known —

                 KAY
    You knew. You knew everything.
```

>   STEVE
> I tried to tell you, I just...
>
>   KAY
> Say it. You just what?

54. USING SUB-HEADERS 💡

Using the advanced formatting technique known as sub-headers can make scripts read faster and clearer. A sub-header is an abbreviated scene heading that can only be used after a full heading has set the scene.

So if you were using this technique during a scene series which takes place in a house, you would have to first do a full INT. LOCATION – TIME heading, for example INT. HOUSE – DAY and then subsequently use HALLWAY, KITCHEN, BEDROOM, etc.

You could use these headers for any room in the house, but would need a full heading when going outside.

55. USING VIRTUAL CLOSE-UPS 💡

Similar to the sub-header is the virtual close-up. A virtual close-up isolates a character's name on its own line to create a close-up in the reader's mind.

This can be a useful tool when trying to keep the geography of characters in a vast space clear.

Here's how a battle might be written using sub-headers and virtual close-ups:

```
EXT. VALLEY — DAY

US Forces line up along the
hillside.  Captain Smith at the
lead.

ACROSS THE VALLEY (sub-header)

The enemy prepares.

BACK AT THE HILLSIDE (sub-header)

Smith surveys his surroundings,
stoic.  And at that moment —

THE ENEMY (virtual close-up)

Charges.

SMITH (virtual close-up)

Gives the signal.

HIS SOLDIERS (virtual close-up)
```

```
Storm downhill, on a collision
course —

THE ENEMY (virtual close-up)

Gains momentum, raising their
Carbines —

IN THE VALLEY (sub-header)

Both sides collide into each other,
kicking up a cloud of dust and gun
smoke and NOISE.
```

56. EXCLAMATION!!!! 💡

Avoid overusing exclamation points, or exclamation marks, or whatever you want to call them. They'll have more impact if you use them sparingly.

57. THE RULES 💡

If your story has magical and supernatural elements, then you must set rules for them right away, usually within the first act. The truth is: this applies to all stories. Every city, job, industry, family and friendship has its rules. They can be anything you want in the script, but once those rules are established, don't break them. You do not want the audience to lose its suspension of disbelief.

For example, if you establish that your zombies don't bleed when shot, don't make them the victims of a bloodbath later in the movie when they're assaulted by an army.

58. USE THE CUT TO CONVEY MEANING 💡

This is not about the actual formatting of the words CUT TO: in the script. This is about how you can tell us a lot by the images you choose to show us. Don't underestimate the power of strong scene transitions.

A lot can be said in a cut that is far more powerful than dialogue. You can match cuts for sound and/or image, or you can counter-balance images. For example, cutting from someone laughing at the end of one scene to someone crying at the start of another.

Use the cut to convey meaning, and the audience will fill in the blanks.

59. OBLIGATORY SCENES 💡

The term "Obligatory Scenes" has a few definitions:

- They can be the most important scenes needed for the plot to work, the scaffolding to the story, the most important beats that make up the structure. You'll want to make sure not to miss any.

- They can also be the necessary scenes required by the expectations an audience has for a genre, such as a bar brawl in a Western, a chase scene in an Action Movie, or the first meeting and first kiss in a Love Story.

- Obligatory scenes can also refer to the payoff scenes required by the setup of your story. For example, if you have a story about a character that grows up with an overbearing father, you need to include a scene in which that character finally stands up to his father. Similarly, if you spend a lot of time setting up an event like a wedding, eventually we will need to see that wedding take place.

60. MIDPOINT 🎵
AKA: Ordeal / Point of No Return / First Culmination / Half-Way Point / The Middle

This is the single most important element to mapping the vast terrain of Act Two. With this beat, you can effectively split Act Two in half, thus giving yourself the challenge of designing two half-hour Sequences as opposed to one sixty-minute Sequence.

In general, the Midpoint is where the stakes are raised, usually by the Lead understanding that the situation is worse than he first imagined. Sometimes in trying to solve the problem, the Lead makes matters worse. This is especially common in a Film Noir and Thriller, but can be applied to all genres.

The Lead can also reach the point where he has come so far, that he is just as close to the end of his journey as he is to the beginning. Some call it the "Point of No Return," because from here on out, the Lead becomes fully committed to solving the problem, whatever the cost.

The stronger you make this moment, the better chance you have of keeping your audience's attention.

61. STATE OF GRACE ⚙⚙

If your Midpoint reflects a moment when your Lead feels he has achieved some sort of victory, it can be followed by what is often called a brief period, or state, of grace. A reward. It can be a page long, it could be ten. This is a moment when your Lead gets a glimpse of what life might be like if he reaches the goal. Think of it as a time to reflect before the journey gets even more difficult. Once in a while, it is found closer to the end of the second act.

62. PRESSURE MOUNTS 🎞

AKA: The Road Back / Bad Guys Close In / Sequence E / Mini-Movie 5

Following the theory of dramatic escalation, it makes sense that if the stakes have been raised and the Lead finds himself in a deeper mess, then this is when we begin to see and feel the vise tightening.

Sometimes the Lead will be recovering from the Midpoint and planning his next move here. When that's the case, we'll see the Lead hiding out. This is a popular time for a romantic scene or sex scene between the Lead and the main love interest.

The Lead will then either perform some sort of reconnaissance on the Opposing Force and make a more ambitious attempt to confront the problem, or the Opposing Force will catch on to the Lead and close in on him or his hideout.

You're on the right path as long as tension (brought on by rising stakes and rising dangers) increases to a near breaking point.

63. TEACHING YOURSELF HOW TO TELL STORIES THROUGH PICTURES 💡

Watch movies without sound. If you can still tell what is happening, the screenwriter and the filmmakers have done their job. Remember, show, don't tell. Behavior and rhythm illustrate the story you want to convey.

Notice how the strongest images are the most primal and the most iconic, the ones that convey a lot with a little, like the classic "picture is worth a thousand words."

64. ANOTHER EXERCISE FOR MASTERING DIALOGUE 💡

Watch movies viewing the subtitles to see how little dialogue is necessary.

65. TRIMMING THE FAT 💡

Test your scenes by removing them from the script, and having the adjacent scenes bump up following each other. If your story stays intact without it, consider removing the scene. The same can be said for any line of dialogue or description.

66. GETTING IN THE MOOD 💡

Try listening to Mozart (or other Classical composers), Miles Davis (or any Jazz), movie scores, or period music while you write. Mozart works for babies, why not for us?

67. KEEPING ACTORS HAPPY 💡

This one's a little heavy. Make sure the character is actually experiencing emotion in a scene, and is taking a position because of it. This ties into the character's wants and needs.

Always ask yourself if you're giving your Lead a strong emotion to play, and a behavior to display it. Don't let him fade into the background.

68. A CLASSIC FORMULA FOR MAKING THE LEAD MORE EMPATHETIC 💡

A trick to make your Lead more compelling or likable is to make the Opposing Force worse. The more we dislike the Opposing Force, the more we will root for the Lead, and become emotionally involved.

69. GETTING THE MOST OUT OF THE SETTING (using location as a character) 🔆

Think about the time and place in which your story occurs. Are you making sure that every city, town, street, building, house, room, and yard adds to the tone? How about the time period?

If you're writing a Thriller, look at how the fog, cobblestone, and gaslight of Victorian England add to the mood of mystery in *Sherlock Holmes* stories. Or how the dirty, wet, neon-drenched streets of New York echo Travis Bickel, and add to the unease in *Taxi Driver*. If you're writing a Romantic Comedy or Caper, are you using locations to enhance the romance, like Paris in *Amelie*, Beverly Hills in *Pretty Woman*, or the Upper West Side in so many Woody Allen films?

Choices about maximizing the impact of the location, in essence making it a character unto itself, are not arbitrary.

Whatever the ultimate choice ends up being, some thought should go into the process. Every word matters in a script and every shot matters in a film. The backdrop the action is set against can go a long way toward giving a film the most visceral impact.

70. FAKE-SOUNDING TALK 💡

Don't overuse a character's name in dialogue. Just think about how often you say your friend's name during a night out or in conversation on the phone - a lot less often than you think.

71. DON'T CONFUSE (O.S.) WITH (V.O.) 💡

O.S. (Off Screen) is when the speaker is still in the scene, but not visible, as in speaking from the next room.

V.O. (Voice Over) is when a person speaks over an image but is not in the scene.

72. FINDING A WAY INTO THE SCENE (SHAKING THINGS UP) 💡

When a scene isn't working, try changing the location, weather, time of day, or maybe even adding or removing a character. Shake things up.

73. EMOTIONAL TRACKING 💡

From time to time, stop and track your Lead through all the scenes you've written. See where he stands emotionally at the end of each scene and if his emotion corresponds to his arc in relation to story structure.

74. STORY IS THE KEY 💡

Focus on story over plot and structure, or any other element. Think of it this way: your story is the heart of what you're trying to say. Your plot is the mechanics of trying to tell that story.

75. THINGS FALL APART 🎵
AKA: Pinch 2 / New Development / All Is Lost / The Death Experience / Reward

A setback occurs that forces the Lead to reexamine his goal, and pushes him to the brink of quitting, if not to quit altogether. Another option is a false triumph, prompting the Lead to think he has solved the problem, but we know he hasn't.

Whichever method you choose, it should look to the audience like matters have spiraled so out of control and the problem has become so grave, that there is no way the Lead will ever be able to fix it, whether the Lead recognizes this or not.

This can happen when the Lead fully realizes the goal of the Opposing Force, or the absolute stakes, often producing an internal and external low point for the Lead. Ironically, this low point may just be the death of old ideas the Lead must shed in order to finally grow.

76. ROCK BOTTOM 🎬
AKA: Lead's Gravest Doubts / Dark Night of the Soul / Crisis / Sequence F / Mini-Movie 6

Like a rain cloud hanging overhead, this big gloom bridges the major realization of "Things Fall Apart" with "The Lead's Choice."

This is an area of doubt, almost mirroring the Deliberation from Act One, but taking into account the larger stakes and the position the Lead finds himself in now.

If you've ever had a moment when you doubted all that you knew, felt there was no way humanly possible to solve your problem, and were forever changed by this moment, you probably know what your Lead is going through.

77. ANOTHER WAY TO IMPROVE YOUR DIALOGUE 💡

Read dialogue out loud. You'll be surprised at how different it sounds. If you can, try to set up a table read with a handful of friends acting the dialogue.

78. YOU GOTTA OWN IT 💡

Any detail that may be deemed a hole or inconsistency in your story that you've glazed over needs to be addressed. Make sure you create clarity in all points of logic within your script.

If there are questions within your script that you can't answer, be prepared to be asked those questions many times down the line.

And a bonus: the best answer will usually be a short one. One or two sentences will indicate clarity.

79. FOR MEN HAVING TROUBLE WRITING WOMEN 💡

There is a trap male writers can fall into when creating female characters. This happens when a female character's goals and actions aren't fully explored, or she gets pigeonholed into a one-dimensional whore or saint role.

For men writing a female character, try writing her as a man, then change the name. Oftentimes, it can be that simple. And who wouldn't want to attract top-caliber talent like Meryl Streep to a script?

80. A GREAT TRICK FOR ADDING CONFLICT THROUGH DIALOGUE 💡

When one character asks another character a question: in the response, try having the respondent refuse to answer, change the subject, ask another question, or lie.

81. TICKING CLOCKS 💡

Does your story merit a ticking clock? Is time an enemy to your Lead? Deadlines often make for compelling story engines.

Think of the bomb in *Speed*, the asteroid in *Armageddon*, the imminent nuptials in *My Best Friend's Wedding*, or even making it back in time for the final question in *Slumdog Millionaire*.

82. ADDING TEXTURE 💡

Try to use colors and textures to add flavor to description and dialogue - remember the reader has been looking at black and white for a while and you are painting a picture.

83. "AS YOU KNOW, JOE..." 💡

This tip started out as a recommendation to keep characters from telling each other things they both obviously know, simply for the audience's benefit. It also applies to not repeating information we already know, so that the best way to cut into a scene when someone has to tell another character something we already know, is to cut in right after the information has been delivered.

However, this also applies to a common problem most often found in Thrillers, when all the important information is revealed to the Lead versus being discovered by the Lead. Avoid having all the exposition necessary to understand your story spewed non-dramatically in one scene toward the end.

The story will be more dynamic if the Lead has followed the clues like breadcrumbs, until one final piece of information makes everything clear. Sometimes the Lead figures it out first, sometimes the audience, sometimes both at the same time. The key is not to heap it all on us at once.

84. COMBINING CHARACTERS 💡

You'll sometimes find that you have too many characters crowding your storyline. Try combining those whose actions are overlapping in moving your Lead's journey forward.

85. SOUND BURSTS 💡

This refers to the formatting of sounds being CAPPED (uppercase) in the script. Write "a shot RINGS out," instead of "a shot rings out." The capped sound adds a POP to the reading experience, giving emphasis in the same way as the sound would on screen.

86. IF YOU'RE LOST IN THE STORY 💡

If you've lost your way, go back to the big questions:

What is this story about? What does my character want right now? What would happen next? What do I want to see?

87. ABUSING PARENTHETICALS 💡

(Limit using parentheticals). Try NOT directing your actors on the page. If you've done a good job setting up the scene and tone through description, you seldom need this device.

You don't want the reader to think you do not have confidence in your storytelling by telling him someone is angry in a parenthetical when she is obviously screaming.

There are some advanced techniques for using parentheticals to clarify subtext, or to show when dialogue is directed from one person to another, but right now make sure that you do not get in the habit of overusing them.

By the way, actors are known for crossing out parentheticals before they read through a script because they find them superfluous.

88. KILL YOUR DARLINGS 💡

If a line or scene is great, but doesn't really serve your story, cut it. Keep a collection in a drawer if it makes you feel better.

89. QUIRKS 💡

Give your character a quirk or a phrase – a specific idiosyncrasy that sets him apart. This is a great way to separate your Lead from the other characters. This also makes him appear consistent through the script.

90. LEAD'S CHOICE 🎵

AKA: Second Plot Point / Second Turning Point / Second Culmination / Peak of Act Two / Act Two Curtain / Act Two Push / Break Into Three

In many stories, the Lead finds himself with a moral dilemma at this point. He can either deal with the issues, reservations, or fears he has about seeing the situation through to the end, or he can cut and run.

Supporting characters or a love interest will often be found in this area, offering a way to escape or a hideaway. The Opposing Force may even be willing to make a deal. Whatever the case, characters are best defined by the decisions they make at times like this.

With his back against a wall, a worthy Lead will make a decision to face up to the challenge once and for all. This is the moment when he transforms from a Lead Character into a Hero.

91. PREPARING FOR THE LAST STAND 🎬
AKA: Sequence G / Mini-Movie 7

The momentum builds in Act Three as the Lead prepares for "The Last Stand," also known as the "Big Showdown" or "Final Confrontation."

Following are some clichéd examples from popular genres:

In Action and War films, we'll see soldiers gear up, load guns, and man planes. In Romantic Comedies, one lover rushes through the city, looking for the love interest she's realized she cannot live without. In Horror films, whoever is left alive will try to set a trap for the killer or monster.

Although all of these examples seem to be overused, the uniqueness that keeps them fresh and embedded in great films are the details each writer brings to his story. And remember, like any of the beats in this guide, a clever writer can always turn them on their head.

92. ENDORPHINS, CONFIDENCE, AND INSPIRATION 💡

Whenever you are really, really blocked, get some fresh air or exercise. Take a long walk or go for a run. The oxygen in your blood will stir your brain activity. This always helps.

93. TONE AND GENRE 💡

Make sure the tone of your writing style matches the genre. This applies to word selection, sentence structure and any other grammatical tool the writer can use to grip us with suspense, make us laugh, or make us cry.

An example from Tony Gilroy's Action/Thriller *The Bourne Ultimatum*:

```
Bourne buys a cell phone. Activates
the SIM card on the new phone.
Dumps the pay-as-you-go package in
a bin. Rounds a corner. Out of
sight.
```

From Alexander Payne & Jim Taylor's Buddy Comedy *Sideways*:

```
Miles grabs the first DIRTY WINE
GLASS he finds and shakes it out as
he approaches the closest tasting
station.  He pushes his way to the
front.

The pourer offers the usual one-
ounce dollop.  Miles jacks it back,
immediately extending his glass for
more.
```

From John Logan's Biopic/Drama *The Aviator*:

```
Noah stands and looks at the
shattered body of what was once
Howard Hughes.

Howard lies in a coma inside his
oxygen tent, connected to chugging
machines.  He has been bandaged,
but the bloody horror is evident.
A whisper of life is all that
remains.

Noah sinks into his chair, looks at
him.
```

94. ENDING WITH THE MOST IMPORTANT WORD 💡

Try to leave the most important or effective word in a description or dialogue sequence for last. It leaves readers with a powerful impression for what's being said or shown, even if they're skimming – which they are known to do.

95. CREATING SUBTLE EMPATHY 💡

By starting line after line with a character's name in a description, the reader is forcefully introduced to a character. As a result, we (the readers and audience) are more likely to stay away from identifying with this character.

Studies have shown the occasional flipping of the subject of a sentence to the second clause will allow readers to ease into a character as opposed to hammering them over and over again with the character's name at the start of each sentence.

For example, "Jack emerges from his bedroom" could be switched to "emerging from the bedroom in a tank top, Jack..." This way, readers emerge with Jack, and you gain a psychological advantage for your Lead.

Avoid overusing this technique. It's not to be done line by line, scene by scene – but most importantly in those first scenes when you introduce the Lead.

96. NO PAYOFF 💡

If you're not finding the right payoff, it's probably because it wasn't set up in the first act. Remember, whatever your Lead isn't capable of doing in the first ten pages, he will be able to do in the last ten pages. In essence, he is shedding his flaw.

97. THE MARKS OF A PRO 💡

Proofread, spell check, and always ask yourself if there is a more emotional way of approaching the story.

98. WRITE FOR THE STAR 💡

It is his movie, since agreeing to attach himself to the project is usually the key to getting it made. Subtly establish him as attractive and give him the best lines.

Also, try to begin and end as many scenes as possible with the star acting or reacting.

99. A CHANGE OF SPACE 💡

Try changing the time of day when you write, where you work, or your writing space itself for variation and a fresh perspective.

100. THE LAST STAND 🎞
AKA: Sequence H / Mini-Movie 8

This is the big, final confrontation when the central conflict of your story must be resolved, and it's no time for compromise. The Lead and the Opposing

Force must face off, with the stakes hanging in the balance.

Your aim should be to make this the biggest, most compelling sequence possible. "The Last Stand" will contain the rest of the beats leading to the Climax of the story.

101. MASTERING YOUR GENRE 💡

Read scripts within the genre you're writing, to see how the pros do it.

102. QUOTE FOR THE DAY 💡

> "The first draft of everything is shit."
>   -Ernest Hemingway

>   (So finish it).

103. GENDER SHIFTS 💡

If the script doesn't seem to gel, consider changing the sex of the Lead.

104. BURYING EXPOSITION 💡

If you want to reveal exposition about the Lead, try having another character say it. Or try revealing it only as a last recourse for the character. The more conflict related to it coming out, or leading to it coming out, the better.

105. YOUR CHARACTERS ARE WHAT THEY EAT 💡

As with everything in stories that originates in real life, you can reveal a lot about characters by what they eat - how, when, and where.

106. PRICELESS PRESTON STURGES TIPS FOR WRITING COMEDY 💡

This from one of the unquestionable master writer/directors of comedy:

"A pretty girl is better than an ugly one. A leg is better than an arm. A bedroom is better than a living room. An arrival is better than a departure. A birth is better than a death. A chase is better than a chat. A dog is better than a landscape. A kitten is better than a dog. A baby is better than a kitten. A kiss is better than a baby. A pratfall is better than anything."

107. FOLLOWING YOUR PASSION 💡

Whenever you're not sure which script to write first of all the ideas you have, choose the one that you'd do if a doctor said you only have six months to live.

108. THE HEART MONITOR 💡

Readers often can tell if they are in for a tough read just by glancing at the pages of screenplay. Large chunks of dialogue and description are usually a good warning sign of a strenuous read ahead. As the writer, here's a small but simple visual test for your pages:

Turn the script on its side, spine down.

Examine the outer margins of your page as if you were looking at a heart-monitor.

If you have consistent spikes, you're alive and well. If you see broad, black, flat stretches, the patient needs to be revived.

109. FORMATTING SINGING (IN MUSICALS) 💡

If you're writing a musical, format the song lyrics as dialogue, but CAP every word.

110. FORMATTING SINGING (IN NON-MUSICALS) 💡

If you're not writing a musical, but want to include song lyrics, write them like normal dialogue within quotation marks.

111. THE OLD SWITCHEROO 💡

If your Lead's dialogue falls flat in a scene, try switching it with the dialogue of the character he's interacting with. Writers have a habit of giving supporting characters the best dialogue.

112. SPONTANEOUS PROSE 💡

When you find yourself overwhelmed by the scene or section you are about to write, try using the stream-of-conscious technique. Usually, once all your fears, hopes and instincts are listed on a page, it's easier to sort through them.

This approach to breaking through a block is preferable to waiting for all the voices in your head to cancel each other out.

113. SUBTEXT 💡

People often say one thing and mean another. The trick to subtext is to have characters say anything except what they really want to say, because dialogue is as much about what people don't say as what they do.

> "…the actual words people use are not nearly as important as the intent behind them."
> -Robert Towne

114. READING IT BACKWARDS 💡

For proofreading, try reading from the back forward, one paragraph at a time, so you are just focusing on the technical aspects and not the context. See how little you actually need to get the message across.

115. THE BLEAKEST MOMENT 🎵

This moment should be the extreme opposite of your Climax. Its purpose is to pull the audience as far in one direction as possible before blasting them back the other way in the Climax.

This is when the Lead, hanging over the side of the cliff, seems just about to let go; when it looks like the Opposing Force is going to get away with what he wants, but doesn't realize he is about to be killed.

116. LEAD REACHES FULL POTENTIAL ♪

Whatever inner flaws have been holding the Lead back the entire story, or whatever tool the Lead had failed to harness at the Midpoint, is taken control of in this moment.

It is only now, by defeating his flaw and harnessing the full potential of what this journey has taught him, that the Lead is finally able to defeat The Opposing Force.

Normally taking up just a few lines in the script at most, this beat's value is priceless as it bridges the Bleakest Moment with the Climax, fulfills the Lead's arc, and makes the final transformation plausible.

The Bleakest Moment plus the Lead Reaching Full Potential equals the Climax.

You know you've pulled this off when the Lead does something at this point that he wouldn't have done before.

117. THE CLIMAX 🎵
AKA: Crest / Summit / Crescendo / Peak / Big Payoff / Finale

This is the moment of highest drama in your story, even if it's a comedy.

By harnessing the special powers the Lead has gained during the course of his adventure, he is finally able to overcome the Opposing Force, save the love interest, stop the World from destruction, and so on.

This is when the Central Question is finally answered.

Sometimes punctuation is added in the form of fireworks, or with the lovers reunited by a kiss, or by the biggest explosion.

118. DENOUEMENT 🎵

Also known as the "Epilogue" or "Falling Action," because the main dramatic tension has been released, this is when all the loose strings of the plot are tied up and we get a gist of where the characters are going from here.

The goal here is to wrap it up as swiftly as possible, because the audience can sense when they're near the end, and they want to go home.

119. FADE OUT IMAGE 🎵

What's the very last image you want the audience to see before the story ends? This is what they'll think of when they walk out of the theater.

You can also use this as a bookend and have it mirror the beginning.

Also, just like the beginning, audio can play a major role. Pay special attention to what will be the last sound said or heard (not including the score).

A well done closing image can ingrain itself into a viewer's memory for years, if not a lifetime.

120. PROTECT YOUR WORK 💡

Don't forget to copyright your script with the US Library of Congress. This is absolutely the best way to protect your work. Go to the link below for more information:

http://www.copyright.gov/help/faq

Screenwriting Terminology Guide

A-Page
A revised page that extends beyond the original page, going onto a second page. (i.e. Page 1, 1A, 2, 3, 3A.)

A-Story
The main thread of the plot, separate from the subplots.

Abbreviations
Shortcuts used in scripts such V.O., O.S.

Above-the-Line
The costs that occur before filming, including salaries of the talent and creative team (director, producer, screenwriter), plus any rights required for adapted scripts. Sometimes, above-the-line can also refer to the people included in the above-the-line payment category.

Act
A large division of a full-length script.

Action
The moving pictures seen on screen. Also, the word spoken by a director indicating that filming begins.

Adaptation
A work based on material originally created for another medium, like books, plays, true stories, graphic novels, TV shows, or toys.

Ad-Lib
Dialogue in which the characters or actors make up what they say in real time on the movie set. From the Latin ad libitum, "in accordance with desire."

Against
A term describing the ultimate potential payday for a writer in a film deal. $400,000 against $800,000 means that the writer is paid $400,000 when the script is finished (through rewrite and polish); when and if the movie goes into production, the writer receives an additional $400,000.

Agent Submission
A method of submission, in which a production company, TV network, or studio requires that a script be submitted by a recognized literary agent.

Alan Smithee
A fictional name taken by a writer or director who doesn't want his real name credited on a film.

Angle
A particular camera placement.

Approved writer
A writer whom a television network trusts to deliver a good script once hired.

Arbitration
Binding adjudication by members of a Writers Guild of America (WGA) committee regarding proper onscreen writer credit of a movie; arbitration is available only to WGA members or potential WGA members.

Attached
Agreement by name actors and/or a director to be a part of the making of a movie.

Audio/Visual Script
A dual column screenplay with video description on the left and audio and dialogue on the right, used in advertising, corporate videos, documentaries and training films.

B-Story
The main subplot of the story, usually a love story or friendship which sheds light on the theme.

b.g.
Abbreviation for "background." (e.g. "In the b.g., kids are fighting.")

Back Door Pilot
A two-hour TV movie that is a setup for a TV series if ratings warrant further production.

Back End
Payment on a movie project when profits are realized.

Back-Story
Experiences of a main character taking place prior to the main action, which contribute to character motivations and reactions.

Bankable
Describing a professional who can get a project financed solely by having his name attached.

Beat
A parenthetically noted pause interrupting dialogue, denoted by (beat), for the purpose of indicating a significant shift in the direction of a scene, much in the way that a hinge connects a series of doors. Also, used to refer to the smallest moments in the story in terms of length, like notes in music. The theory of descending structure in screenplays is: the Whole Story, the Individual Acts that make up the

story, the Sequences within the Acts, the Scenes within the Sequences, and the Beats within the Scenes.

Beat Sheet
An abbreviated description of the main events in a screenplay or story.

Binding
What literally holds the script together. A writer submitting a manuscript might use either brads with cardstock covers or one of a number of other pre-made folders, available from WritersStore.com.

Board
A corkboard or blackboard used for outlining a story using index cards.

Bookend
The technique of opening with an event that occurs later in the story, then flashing back and playing out the story, only to again return to the event – usually somewhere toward the end.

Brads
Brass fasteners used to bind a screenplay printed on three-hole punched paper. Acco #5 solid brass brads are generally accepted as having the highest quality.

Bump
A troublesome element in a script that negatively deflects the reader's attention away from the story.

Button
A TV writing term (that has made its way into feature films) referring to a witty line that tops off a scene. See Tip # 40.

Buyer
A gatekeeper with the power to green-light the purchase or production of a project. In other words, a person with the power to say "yes."

C-Story
The main character's internal journey dealing with his flaw and leading to his eventual arc or lack thereof.

Cable
A cable television network such as HBO, or cable television in general.

Cards
Index cards, usually sized 3" x 5" that are used for outlining stories on a cork board or within digital outlining software.

Cast
The characters who are physically present in the film. These are the roles for which actors will be needed. A role in a film described as being double-cast with another means that the same actor is expected to play both roles (e.g. Eddie Murphy in *The Nutty Professor*).

CGI
Computer Generated Image; a term denoting that computers will be used to generate the full imagery.

Character
Any personified entity appearing in a film.

Character Arc
The emotional progress of the characters during the story. Usually the chief tool used by the writer to illustrate a story's theme.

Character Cue
When a character speaks, his name appears on the line preceding the dialogue. In screenplays, the name is tabbed to a location that is roughly in the center of the line.

Cheat a Script
Fudging the margins and spacing of a screenplay on a page (usually with a software program) in an attempt to fool the reader into thinking the script is

shorter than it really is. Some programs refer to this as "Leading."

Close Up
A very close camera angle on a character or object.

Complication
The second act of a three-act dramatic structure, in which "the plot thickens," peaking at its end.

Conflict
The heart of drama; someone wants something and people and things keep getting in the way of him achieving the goal. At times, the obstacles can be common to both the hero and villain, and the ultimate goal a laudable one for both parties.

Continuing Dialogue
Dialogue spoken by the same character that continues uninterrupted onto the next script page.

Continuous Action
Included in the scene heading when moving from one scene to the next, as the action continues.

Copyright
Proof of ownership of an artistic property that comes with registration of a script through the United States Register of Copyrights.

Copyright Notice
Placing "© Your Name" on the Title Page of a script.

Courier 12 Pitch
The main font in use in the U.S. by both publishers and the Hollywood film industry.

Coverage
The notes prepared by script readers at a literary agency, film production company, or script competition. Coverage is typically divided into three sections: plot synopsis and evaluation, the discussion of the quality of the writing, and a recommendation that either passes on the script or kicks it on to the next level. Typically, coverage is for internal use and almost never shared with the writer.

Creative Executive
(Or "Creative Exec" or "Studio Exec")
Evaluates literary material to determine whether his/her company should option or purchase the property. Literary material usually needs to be recommended by a reader before the Exec will look it. The Exec may also help guide the project through the development process. Though no longer used (for politically correct reasons), Execs are sometimes still referred to by the term "D-Girl" or "Development Girl," a holdover from the old studio

days when this position was almost exclusively filled by women.

Deal Memo
A contractual agreement that defines the specific terms for an assignment, be it between a writer and a producer or company, or between members of a writing team.

Development
The process of preparing a script for production.

Development Hell
The dreaded creative malaise that sets in when the development process lasts too long.

Dialogue
The speech by or between characters in a film.

Dialogue Pass
A rewrite or polish of a script solely focused on improving the dialogue.

Director
In film, the individual responsible for staging (i.e. placing in the space or "blocking") the actors, sculpting and coordinating their performances, and making sure they fit with the design elements into a coherent vision of the script, (e.g. choosing the shot list).

Draft
A version of a screenplay. Each draft of a rewrite/revision is numbered differently.

Dual Dialogue
When two characters speak simultaneously; see also "Simultaneous Dialogue."

Dual Protagonists
Having more than one protagonist in a story. In Hollywood, this is called having "dual protagonists" or a "two-hander."

Emphasized Dialogue
Dialogue the writer wants stressed, usually identified with italics.

Establishing Shot
A cinematic shot that establishes a certain location or area.

Exposition
The first act of dramatic structure, in which the main conflict and characters are exposed or revealed. Also, any information about the characters, conflict or world of the story.

EXT.
Outdoors.

Extension
A technical note placed directly to the right of the character's name that denotes how his voice is heard. For example, O.S. is an extension that stands for Off-Screen.

f.g.
Abbreviation for "foreground." (e.g. "In the f.g., kids are fighting.")

Feature Film
A movie made primarily for distribution in theaters, usually between 90-120 minutes in length.

Film Festival
A festival of short and/or feature-length films shown over a few days or a few weeks. Festivals are places for films and filmmakers to gain exposure and critical buzz and, in many cases, distribution. The two best-known festivals in the world are Sundance and Cannes.

First-Look Deal
An agreement between a writer or a director with a production company (or a production company with a studio) in which the company (or studio) has the right to purchase or produce any new project. Only after the production company or studio has passed can the project be submitted for consideration

elsewhere. These deals are usually reserved for writers and filmmakers with proven track records.

FLASHBACK
A scene from the past that interrupts the action to explain motivation or reaction of a character to the immediate scene.

Font
The look of the printed text on the page. For screenplays, Courier 12 point is the standard (a fixed font which in practical terms means that an l or an M, although the M being wider, occupy the same width of space).

Formula
Usually refers to a sure-fire method of structuring a script (i.e. it must include certain elements and arrive at a certain ending). For example, there have been a slew of movies where a group of misfits are thrown together and ultimately become the David that slays Goliath on the athletic field (e.g. *The Bad News Bears*).

Four-Act Structure
Dividing the second act in half, thus breaking the story into four quarters or acts.

FREEZE FRAME
The image on the screen stops, freezes and becomes a still shot.

Genre
The category a story or script falls into - such as: Thriller, Comedy, Drama, Romantic Comedy, Romance, Action, Action-Adventure, Western, Epic, Horror, Bio-Pic, Fantasy, Sci-Fi, Musical, Satire, Dramedy, Dark Comedy, Mystery (Whodunit), and many others.

Green
A writer or draft of a script that is raw, rough, or underdeveloped and needs more work before being of a professional caliber.

Green-Light
A company or studio's approval which allows a project to move out of development and into production.

Header
An element of a Production Script occupying the same line as the page number, which is on the right and .5" from the top. Printed on every script page, header information includes the date of a revision and the color of the page.

Heat
Positive gossip about a project through the Hollywood grapevine.

High Concept
A brief statement of a movie's basic idea that is felt to have tremendous public appeal.

Hip Pocket
A casual relationship with an established agent in lieu of a signed, formal agreement of representation.

Hook
A term borrowed from songwriting that describes that thing that catches the public's attention and keeps them interested in the flow of a story.

Indie
A production company independent of major film studio financing.

INT.
Indoors.

Intercut
A script instruction denoting that the action moves back and forth between two or more scenes.

Interrupt
When one character cuts off another character's dialogue, sometimes marked with ellipses (...) but better marked with an em dash (—).

Line Reading
When a director gives an actor direction of a specific way to perform a line of dialogue.

Literary Office
Usually headed by the literary manager and often staffed with interns and in-house or freelance readers. Typically the place to direct script submissions and inquiries.

Locked Pages
A software term for finalized screenplay pages that are handed out to the department heads and talent in preparation for production. Further changes are only made via A and B Pages (see above).

Logline
A 25 words or less description of a screenplay. Four things to keep in mind: Who is the story about? What does he want? What gets in his way? What is the dramatic irony? The logline is the answer when people ask "what is your story about?" It's a great logline if their eyes light up and they want to hear more.

Low Concept
The opposite of "High Concept" – an idea or slice-of-life story that seems to have limited commercial appeal. Also known as a "tough sell."

Lyrics
The words that are sung by characters in a musical.

M.O.S.
Without sound; an expression attributed to a German-speaking director who wanted a scene with no sound. He instructed his crew to shoot "mit out sound."

Master Scene Script
A script formatted without scene numbering (the usual format for a spec screenplay).

Match Cut
A transition in which something in the scene that follows in some way directly matches a character or object in the previous scene.

Meet-and-Greet
Usually the first meeting between a writer and an executive (or a writer and a potential representative) when the focus is on getting to know each other and establishing a relationship that may bear fruit on future projects. This is opposed to a pitch meeting

where the focus is on buying or selling a specific script or story.

Miniseries
A long-form movie of three hours or more shown on successive nights or weeks on a television network.

Montage
A cinematic device used to show a series of scenes, all related and building to some conclusion.

Movie of the Week
Also known as a "MOW," a movie made primarily for broadcast on a television or cable network.

Multimedia
Writing and filmmaking encompassing more than one medium at a time which, script-wise, usually refers to CD-ROM games or Internet-based programming.

Multiple Casting
When an actor plays more than one character.

Musical
A story in which songs and music are an integral part of the dramatic structure.

Notes
Ideas about a screenplay shared with a screenwriter by someone responsible for moving the script forward into production, which the screenwriter is generally expected to use to revise the screenplay. A writer can also hire consultants to receive feedback (notes) to help improve the script, prior to submitting it to an agent, manager, or production company.

Numbered Scenes
Numbers that appear to the right and left of the scene heading to aid the Assistant Director in breaking down the scenes for scheduling and production.

O.C.
Abbreviation for Off Camera, denoting that the speaker is resident within the scene but not seen by the camera.

O.S.
Abbreviation for Off Screen, denoting that the speaker is not resident within the scene.

One-Hour Episodic
A screenplay for a television show whose episodes fill a one-hour time slot, week to week.

Opening Credits
Onscreen text describing the most important people involved in the making of a movie.

Option
The securing of the rights to a screenplay for a given length of time.

Outline
A breakdown of a story, scene-by-scene, (anywhere from 2 to 80 pages) that the writer will use as a roadmap for writing an upcoming draft. Usually longer than a Beat Sheet, which only focuses on the most important moments. Usually more technical than a Treatment, which attempts to be an entertaining read in the spirit of the script.

Package
The assembly of the basic elements necessary to secure financing for a film.

PAN
A camera direction indicating a stationary camera that pivots back and forth or up and down.

Parenthetical
An inflection on the speech of a character, as directed by a writer. Also known as a "wryly" because of the propensity of amateur screenwriters to try to accent a character's speech, as in:

```
          BOB (wryly)
     Well, isn't that special?
```

Pass
A rejection of a property by a potential producer or an agent.

Pitch
To verbally describe a property to a potential buyer in the hope it will be bought.

Points
Percentage participation in the profits of a film.

Polish
In theory, to rewrite a few scenes in a script to improve them. In practice, a screenwriter is often expected to do a complete rewrite of a script for the price of a polish.

POV
Point of View; a camera angle placed so as to seem that the camera is the eyes of a character.

Producer
The person or entity financially responsible for a film production.

Production Script
A script in which no more major changes or rewrites are anticipated to occur, which is used day-by-day for filming on a movie set.

Professional Recommendation
A method of submission in which a writer may submit a full script if it's accompanied by a reference.

Project Slate
All the scripts currently in development for which an executive is responsible. (From the book *Breakfast with Sharks* by Michael Lent.)

Property
Any intellectual property in any form (including a play or screenplay) that might form the basis of a movie.

Purchase Contract
A legal agreement with a production company or studio in which the writer sells all rights to a spec screenplay for a negotiated price, usually with more money promised if the project actually moves into production.

Query
A method of submission in which a writer approaches an agent, manager, or producer with a brief introduction letter, also containing a logline or a synopsis.

Reader (AKA Script Reader)
A person who reads screenplays for a production company and writes a report about them, often being paid per report.

Reading
A performance of a script in which the actors are script-in-hand. It could either take place around a table (called a table reading) or with some blocking or staging (a staged reading).

Register of Copyrights
The US government office that registers intellectual property (e.g. scripts), necessary prior to filing a claim for copyright infringement in court.

Release
A legal document given to unrepresented writers for signing by agents, producers or production companies, absolving said entities of legal liability.

Resolution
The third act of a dramatic structure, in which the conflict comes to some kind of conclusion: the protagonist either gets it or doesn't.

Reversal
A place in the plot where a character achieves the opposite of his aim, resulting in a change from good fortune to bad fortune.

Revised Pages
Changes are made to the script after the initial circulation of the Production Script, which are different in color and incorporated into the script without displacing or rearranging the original, unrevised pages.

Riffing
Taken from music; brainstorming.

Romantic Comedy
Also known as a "Romcom," a comedic movie in which the main story revolves around a romance.

Sale
The actual purchase by a producer or studio to the rights of a script written on spec.

Scene
Action taking place in one location and in a distinct time that moves the story to the next element.

Scene Heading
A short description of the location and time of day of a scene, also known as a "slugline." For example: EXT. MOUNTAIN CABIN - DAY would denote that the action takes place outside a mountain cabin during daylight hours.

Screening
The showing of a film for test audiences and/or people involved in the making of the movie.

Screenplay Contest
A submission opportunity for screenwriters in which a group of judges select one or more winners from the entered scripts. Typically, contests require entry fees of around $40-$50, but can often result in prizes as high as $20,000 or more for the winner(s), as well as important exposure to agents and production companies. Some fellowship opportunities effectively function as contests (e.g. Nicholl), choosing a handful of fellows from the pool of entrants.

Screenwriter
The most important and most abused person in Hollywood. The screenwriter writes the script that

provides the foundation for the film, though it may go through any number of changes, both in the rewriting process before production, during production, and in the editing process afterward. In film, there may be many screenwriters throughout the life of a project.

Screenwriting
The art of writing scripts for a visual medium.

Script
The blueprint or roadmap that outlines a movie story through visual descriptions, actions of characters, and their dialogue. The term "script" also applies to teleplays.

Script Cover
What protects the script on travels between the writer and potential readers. The Writers Store carries a number of acceptable covers.

Script Reader
See also "Reader."

Scriptwriting Software
Computer software designed specifically to format and aid in the writing of screenplays and teleplays.

Set
The physical elements that are constructed or arranged to create a sense of place.

Setting
The time and place of a screenplay.

Sequences
This goes back to the early days of film when it took several minutes for a projectionist to switch reels when showing a film. The Sequences were used as a bridge from one major beat to the next. They usually built to a cliffhanger that kept the audience interested while the reels were switched. Many scripts prior to 1950 used to list the sequences on the first page. Author and Professor Paul Gulino can be credited with reintroducing it to a new generation of writers.

SFX
Abbreviation for Sound Effects.

Shooting Script
A script that has been prepared to be put into production.

Shot
What the camera sees. For example, TRACKING SHOT would mean that the camera is following a character as he walks in a scene. WIDE SHOT

would mean that we see every character that appears in the scene, all at once. Shots are rarely, if ever, included in spec scripts.

Showrunner
A writer/producer ultimately responsible for the production of a TV series week-to-week.

Simultaneous Dialogue
When two characters speak at the same time, written in two columns side by side, also known as "Dual Dialogue."

Situation Comedy
Also known as a "Sitcom," a normally 30-minute (in the United States) comedic television show revolving around funny situations the main characters repeatedly fall into.

Slugline
Another name for a SCENE HEADING.

SMASH CUT
A quick or sudden cut from one scene to another.

Soap Opera
Daytime dramas so named because they were originally sponsored by the makers of laundry detergent in the early days of television.

Spec Script
A script written without being commissioned on the speculative hope that it will be sold.

SPFX
Abbreviation for Special Effects.

Spitballing
Another term for brainstorming.

Split Screen
A screen with different scenes taking place in two or more sections; the scenes are usually interactive, as in the depiction of two sides of a phone conversation.

Stock Shot
A sequence of film previously shot and available for purchase and use from a film library.

Story-Type
Sometimes referred to as "genre," or "sub-genre," it can also mean the key element of the story, such as: Coming-of-Age, Fish-Out-of-Water, Supernatural, Buddy, Quest, Underdog, Wedding, Body-Switch, Dysfunctional-Family, Screwball, Slapstick, Raunchy, Spy, Gangster, Crime, Cop, Heist or Caper, Urban, Slasher, Christmas, Torture-Porn, Holiday, Family, Chase, Disaster, War, Ensemble, Chick Flick, Sports, Teen Flick, Kid Flick and Indie.

Pairing a genre with a story-type sets up the writer to pinpoint his type of story, e.g. "Coming-of-Age Comedy," "Gangster-Biopic," "Indie-Dramedy."

Submission
Name for a script once it is submitted to producers, agents, or managers.

SUPER
Abbreviation for "superimpose" meaning the laying of one image on top of another, usually words over a filmed scene (e.g. Berlin, 1945). Also interchangeable with terms such as: LEGEND, CAPTION, or TITLE. The similar TITLE CARD is used when the text is superimposed over a BLACK SCREEN.

Synopsis
A two to three-page double-spaced description of a screenplay.

Tag
A short scene at the end of a movie that usually provides some upbeat addition to the climax or a sinister loose end that hints at a sequel, as in many horror films.

Technical Demands
The extent to which a screenplay requires specific lighting, sound, sets, etc. Screenplays with minimal

technical demands are easier and less expensive to produce.

The Business
Show business in general; more specifically, Hollywood moviemaking and television business.

Thriller
A fast-paced, high-stakes story in which the protagonist is generally in danger at every turn, with the biggest threat coming in the final confrontation with the antagonist.

Ticking Clock
A dramatic device in which some event looming in the near future requires that the conflict reach a speedy resolution (hence, the ticking clock).

TITLE
Text that appears onscreen denoting a key element of the movie, a change of location or date (see SUPER), or person involved in the making of the movie.

Title Page
A page of the script that contains the title and the author's contact information.

Tracking Board
A private industry-only chat room where executives can follow a project's development or status, or share thoughts on a spec currently making the rounds.

Trades
Term used for the daily periodicals covering the news and events of the film and television industries. The two most popular are *Daily Variety* and *The Hollywood Reporter*.

Transition
A script notation denoting an editing transition within the telling of a story. For example, DISSOLVE TO: means the action seems to blur and refocus into another scene, and is generally used to imply a passage of time.

Treatment
A scene-by-scene description of a screenplay, minus all or most of the dialogue.

Turning Point
The most important events in the story. There is no exact number or limit for Turning Points in a script. Terms like "Major Events," "Major Beats," "Plot Points," and "Turning Points" are often interchangeable. Blake Snyder suggests 15, John Truby 22, Vicki King 9, Stanley Kubrick spoke of 6.

Turnaround
The act in which a company or studio decides enough time has been spent trying to move a project into production, and essentially ends up offering to sell the rights to any buyer willing to cover development costs up to that point.

Tweak
A minor change made in a scene or portion of a screenplay.

Unsolicited Script
A method of script submission in which the writer sends the script, without prior contact, to an agency or production company. Some agencies allow this, most don't, and very few film production companies, for liability reasons, will read unsolicited materials.

V.O.
Abbreviation for Voice Over, denoting that the speaker is narrating the action onscreen.

Voice
A writer's unique world view, choice of material, and/or writing style that separates him from everyone else. One of the qualities that cannot be taught, but must be honed in order for a writer to be considered unique, developed, or special. It's what

makes him better at telling a given story than anyone else.

Weekend Read
A script, usually part of a pile ranging from 5 to 30 potential projects, that Executives read on their time off from Friday to Sunday. An opinion on all of these reads is usually expected by the Monday morning meeting between the Executives and their bosses.

WGA Signatory
An agent, producer or production company who has signed an agreement to abide by established agreements with the Writers Guild of America.

Workshop
A developmental production of a screenplay, with a significant amount of rehearsal, but with less fully realized production values (e.g. set) than a full production.

Writers Guild of America
Also known as "the WGA." The main union for screenwriters in the United States, with chapters in Los Angeles (WGAw) and New York (WGAe).

Writing Assignment
A job taken by a writer to rewrite or polish a script originally written by another writer, or to adapt a

work from another medium into a screenplay. Unlike a spec, the writer accepting the assignment knows he will be paid for his work upfront.

Recommended Books for Further Reading

Expand your knowledge of screenwriting and build your reference library with these top books on the craft. The selection below represents the guides we've found the most helpful, and all of them are available at great prices on WritersStore.com.

General Screenwriting and Structure

>**Screenplay: The Foundations of Screenwriting** by Syd Field

>**The Screenwriter's Workbook** by Syd Field

>**Save the Cat!** by Blake Snyder

>**Save the Cat! Goes to the Movies** by Blake Snyder

>**How to Write a Movie in 21 Days: The Inner Movie Method** by Viki King

>**The Writer's Journey: Mythic Structures for Writers** by Christopher Vogler

>**Screenwriting: The Sequence Approach** by Paul Joseph Gulino

The Screenwriter's Bible: A Complete Guide to Writing, Formatting, and Selling Your Script by David Trottier

Making Movies by Sidney Lumet

The Art of Adaptation: Turning Fact and Fiction into Film by Dr. Linda Seger

The Elements of Style for Screenwriters: The Essential Manual for Writers of Screenplays by Paul Argentini

The Hollywood Standard: The Complete & Authoritative Guide to Script Format and Style by Christopher Riley

Rewriting

Writing for Emotional Impact: Advanced Dramatic Techniques to Attract, Engage, and Fascinate the Reader from Beginning to End by Karl Iglesias

Rewrite: A Step-By-Step Guide to Strengthening Structure, Characters, and Drama by Paul Chitlik

Making a Good Script Great by Dr. Linda Seger

The Screenwriter's Problem Solver by Syd Field

Character and Theme

The Art of Dramatic Writing by Lajos Egri

Creating Unforgettable Characters by Dr. Linda Seger

Inside Story: The Power of the Transformational Arc by Dara Marks

The Complete Writer's Guide to Heroes and Heroines: 16 Master Archetypes by Tami D. Cowden, Sue Viders, Carolyn Lafever

The Business

Breakfast with Sharks by Michael Lent

Adventures in the Screen Trade by William Goldman

Which Lie Did I Tell?: More Adventures in the Screen Trade by William Goldman

Good in a Room: How to Sell Yourself (and Your Ideas) and Win Over Any Audience by Stephanie Palmer

The 101 Habits of Highly Successful Screenwriters by Karl Iglesias

Easy Riders, Raging Bulls: How the Sex-Drugs-And-Rock-N-Roll Generation Saved Hollywood by Peter Biskind

Down and Dirty Pictures: Miramax, Sundance, and the Rise of Independent Film by Peter Biskind

The Script-Selling Game: A Hollywood Insider's Look at Getting Your Script Sold and Produced by Kathie Fong Yoneda

Bambi vs. Godzilla: On the Nature, Purpose, and Practice of the Movie Business by David Mamet

Secrets of the Screen Trade by Allen B. Ury